Dear Parent:
Your child's love of reading

Every child learns to read in a different way and ___ own
speed. Some go back and forth between reading ___ read
favorite books again and again. Others read throug_. each level in
order. You can help your young reader improve and become more
confident by encouraging his or her own interests and abilities. From
books your child reads with you to the first books he or she reads
alone, there are I Can Read Books for every stage of reading:

SHARED READING
Basic language, word repetition, and whimsical illustrations,
ideal for sharing with your emergent reader

BEGINNING READING
Short sentences, familiar words, and simple concepts
for children eager to read on their own

READING WITH HELP
Engaging stories, longer sentences, and language play
for developing readers

READING ALONE
Complex plots, challenging vocabulary, and high-interest topics
for the independent reader

ADVANCED READING
Short paragraphs, chapters, and exciting themes
for the perfect bridge to chapter books

I Can Read Books have introduced children to the joy of reading
since 1957. Featuring award-winning authors and illustrators and a
fabulous cast of beloved characters, I Can Read Books set the
standard for beginning readers.

A lifetime of discovery begins with the magical words **"I Can Read!"**

*Visit www.icanread.com for information
on enriching your child's reading experience.*

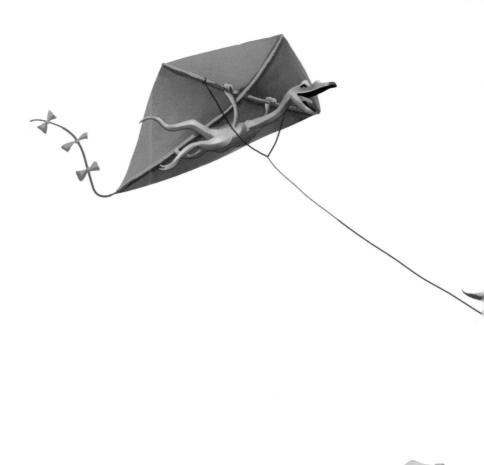

I Can Read!

READING
2
WITH HELP

DIZZY DINOSAURS
SILLY DINO POEMS

edited by **LEE BENNETT HOPKINS**
illustrated by **BARRY GOTT**

HARPER
An Imprint of HarperCollinsPublishers

Acknowledgments

Thanks are due to the following for use of works in this collection:

Curtis Brown, Ltd. for "Prayer of Triceratops" by Rebecca Kai Dotlich. Copyright © 2011 by Rebecca Kai Dotlich; "After the Bath" and "Oops!" by Lee Bennett Hopkins. Copyright © 2011 by Lee Bennett Hopkins. All reprinted by Curtis Brown, Ltd.

Kristy Dempsey for "Dinosaur History" and "Picky Eater." Used by permission of the author, who controls all rights.

Douglas Florian for "Deinocheirus." Used by permission of the author, who controls all rights.

Joan Bransfield Graham for "When Dinosaurs Dance." Used by permission of the author, who controls all rights.

Sarah Hansen for "Picture Day" and "School Rules." Used by permission of the author, who controls all rights.

Michele Krueger for "Lunchtime, Crunch Time" and "Pterodactyl Pilot." Used by permission of the author, who controls all rights.

Linda Kulp for "Saltopus." Used by permission of the author, who controls all rights.

Laura Purdie Salas for "Acrocanthosaurus." Used by permission of the author, who controls all rights.

Lawrence Schimel for "Back-to-School Sale." Used by permission of the author, who controls all rights.

Marilyn Singer for "Tricera-Flops." Used by permission of the author, who controls all rights.

Ann Rousseau Smith for "Dino School Bus." Used by permission of the author, who controls all rights.

Amy Ludwig VanDerwater for "Bathtime." Used by permission of the author, who controls all rights.

Anthony G. Venturi for "Dinosaur Games." Used by permission of the author, who controls all rights.

Allan Wolf for "Velociraptor Rap." Used by permission of the author, who controls all rights.

Library of Congress Cataloging-in-Publication Data is available.
ISBN 978-0-06-135839-5 (trade bdg.) — ISBN 978-0-06-135841-8 (pbk.)

*To Connor Anthony Bice
and his grandfather
—L.B.H.*

*For Rose, Finn, and Nandi
—B.G.*

Contents

How to Say Dinosaur Names

Acrocanthosaurus (AK-roh-CAN-thuh-SAWR-us)

Brachyceratops (BRACK-i-SER-a-tops)

Carcharodontosaurus (Kahr-KAR-o-DON-to-SAWR-us)

Deinocheirus (DINE-oh-KIE-rus)

Hadrosaurus (HAD-ruh-SAWR-us)

Pachycepholosaurus (PAK-ee-SEF-a-loh-SAWR-us)

Pterodactyl (ter-roh-DACT-ill)

Saltopus (SAL-toh-pus)

Sauropod (SAWR-o-pod)

Torosaurus (tor-oh-SORE-us)

Triceratops (tri-SER-uh-tops)

Tyrannosaurus rex (tye-RAN-oh-SAWR-us recks)

Velociraptor (ve-LOSS-oh-RAP-tor)

Tricera-Flops

by Marilyn Singer

Triceratops wakes and every morn,
polishes his horn, horn, horn.

He promises to keep each clean,
free of mud and bits of green.

Yet somehow by 11:30,
Triceratops is good and dirty.

At playing hard, this dino's tops.
At staying neat—Tricera-flops!

Back-to-School Sale

by Lawrence Schimel

Clothes for every dinosaur,

No matter shape or size.

We have a wide selection—

You won't believe your eyes.

Shirts with room for spikes.

Pants with holes for tails.

Torosaurus turtlenecks.

They're all on sale!

The hottest dino styles
For the hippest dinosaurs.
The latest fall fashions—
Now in DinoStores.

Dino School Bus

by Ann Rousseau Smith

Our bus is wide
from side to side,
with room for all,
both short and tall.

We climb the bus
each one of us,
with horns, scales,
and clublike tails.

With spikes and humps
we roll and bump
to reach our school
where dinos rule.

School Rules

by Sarah Hansen

No chomping

No romping

No treading on tails

No clawing

No climbing

No gnawing your nails

No roaring

No soaring

No sharpening teeth

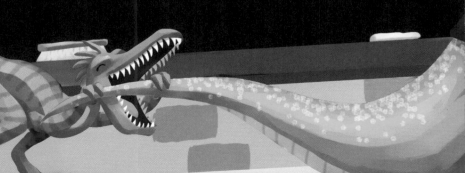

No stamping

No stalking

Small friends to eat

These are rules

All dinos must follow

They keep school safe—

So no one gets swallowed!

Picture Day

by Sarah Hansen

Spikes glossed

Teeth flossed

Claws clipped

Domes tipped

Sit up straight

Look first-rate

Tails tucked in

Reptiles *GRIN*

Hooray! Hooray!

It's Pachycepholosaurus

Perfect

Picture day!

19

Dinosaur Games

by Anthony G. Venturi

It was hard
for Hadrosaurus
to play hide-and-seek.

Too hard to hide
    a long, long tail.
Too hard to hide
    a duck-billed head.

So all they did
the whole day long
was play
touch-tag
instead.

Pterodactyl Pilot

by Michele Krueger

At school I learn to spread my wings
to catch a morning breeze.

I'm a Pterodactyl pilot
gliding through the trees.

I am swooping—
    looping in the air.

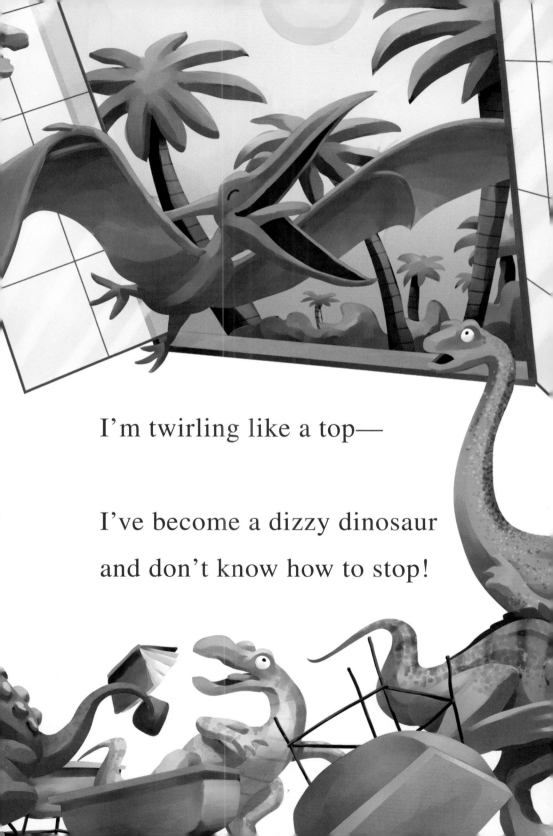

I'm twirling like a top—

I've become a dizzy dinosaur
and don't know how to stop!

Acrocanthosaurus

by Laura Purdie Salas

I can spell

jaws

claws

I can spell

hunt

grunt

I can spell

flame

name

24

But—

I cannot spell

my

long

long

name.

HELLO, MY NAME IS
Akronachlos
Arca Acroth
Acorcathansaur

Lunchtime, Crunch Time

by Michele Krueger

A bully is in the schoolyard.

His name?

TYRANNOSAURUS.

My friends say:

    "Stay away from him.

    Let's hope he will ignore us."

Never poke or pinch him.

Never ask him for a favor.

At lunch, T. rex might just find out
YOU are his favorite flavor.

Picky Eater

by Kristy Dempsey

"A burger, sir, without the bread,"
　　the timid T. rex sweetly said.
"Oh, no, I do not care for cheese
and hold the lettuce, if you please.
Tomatoes make my belly ache
and onions cause my scales to flake.
Just the meat is what I chew—
So, hurry, sir, or
　　　I'll eat you!"

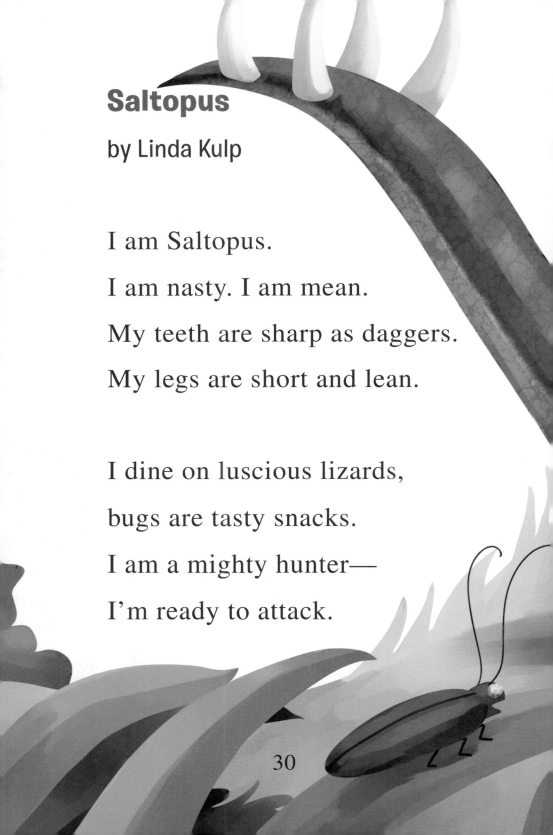

Saltopus

by Linda Kulp

I am Saltopus.

I am nasty. I am mean.

My teeth are sharp as daggers.

My legs are short and lean.

I dine on luscious lizards,

bugs are tasty snacks.

I am a mighty hunter—

I'm ready to attack.

I am Saltopus.

My brain is rather small.

I could be a Dino King—

But I'm just one foot

tall.

When Dinosaurs Dance

by Joan Bransfield Graham

When dinosaurs dance,
  they groove to the beat
by thumping their tails,
  then stamping their feet.

They
  rock,
  roar,
  and roll.

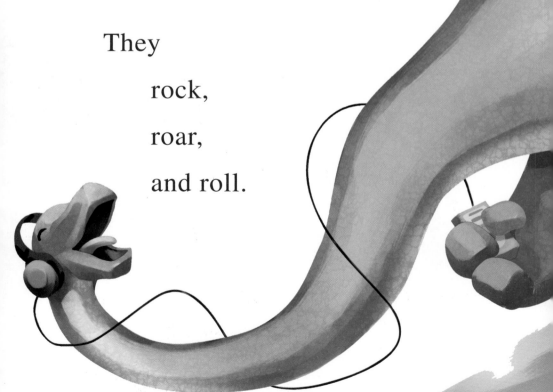

They

 shake,

 shimmy,

 romp—

learning new steps to the

 SAUROPOD STOMP!

33

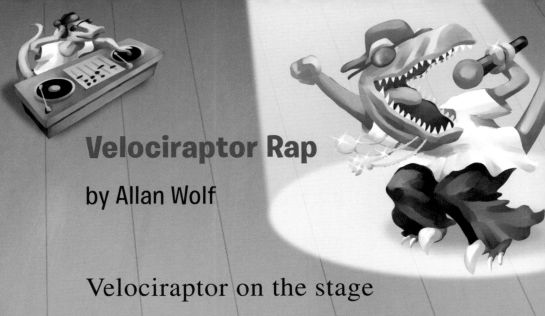

Velociraptor Rap

by Allan Wolf

Velociraptor on the stage
with his rockin' raptor band.
Velociraptor all the rage.
Microphone in raptor hand.

Velociraptor, saggy pants,
golden chains and baseball cap.
Make the dizzy dinos dance.
Rap, Velociraptor, rap!

Deinocheirus

by Douglas Florian

Deinocheirus came to dinner.

He sat down in a chair.

He was so rude—

Ate all the food,

And his friends' best silverware.

35

Oops!

by Lee Bennett Hopkins

When

    Carcharodontosaurus's
    tooth popped out,
he shouted:

    "How could this possibly
    come about?

    I can no longer chew meat.
    I *hate* nibbling plants.

I'll just sit here forever—and pout!"

Bathtime

by Amy Ludwig VanDerwater

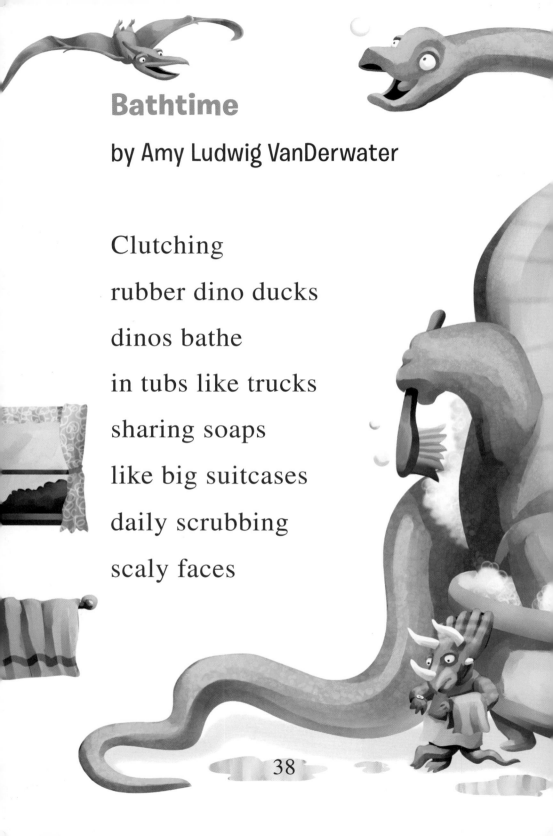

Clutching

rubber dino ducks

dinos bathe

in tubs like trucks

sharing soaps

like big suitcases

daily scrubbing

scaly faces

dinos bob

in beach ball bubbles

forgetting their

ENORMOUS

troubles.

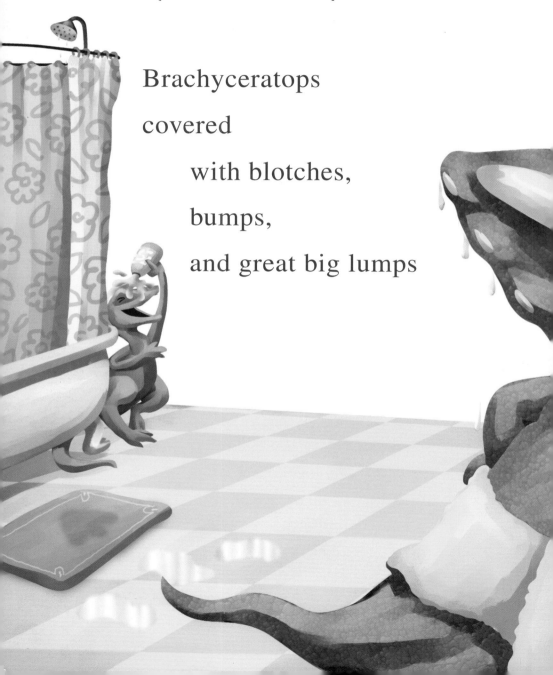

After the Bath

by Lee Bennett Hopkins

Brachyceratops

covered

   with blotches,

   bumps,

   and great big lumps

doesn't have a notion

where

he put his jar of

Baby-Dino-Soft-Skin-Lotion.

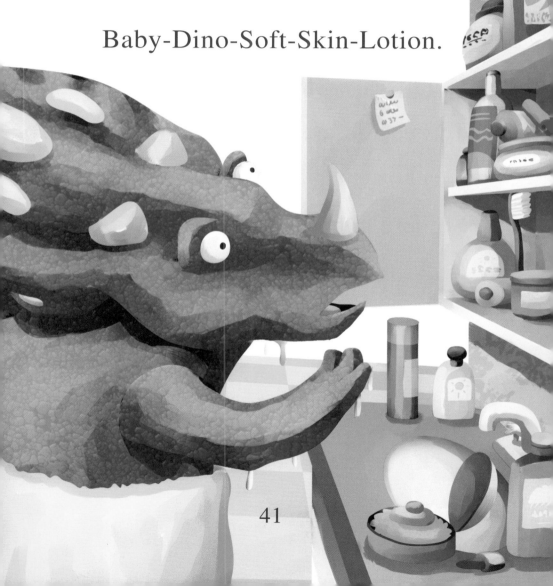

Prayer of Triceratops

by Rebecca Kai Dotlich

Now I stand me up to sleep.

I pray to stars my horns to keep.

Hear this wish—I need all three

To keep T. rex from gobbling me.

So here's the thing

I roar to you—

Bless *this* horn . . .

And *this* one, too.

And *this* one, too.

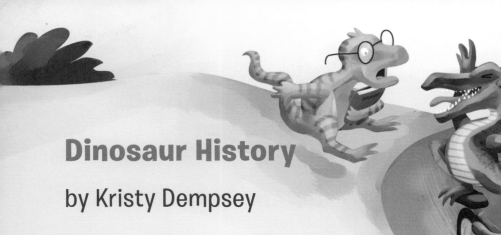

Dinosaur History

by Kristy Dempsey

When dinosaurs were little tikes,
they rode their tiny dino bikes
without a helmet down the street
standing up atop the seat.

They played in dino swimming pools
but never followed water rules.
They would not go to bed on time
Or take a bath to wash off grime.

They always disobeyed their mothers,
rudely crossed their eyes at others.
In the end, their luck went bust . . .
those carefree dinos

BIT

THE

DUST!

Index of Authors and Titles

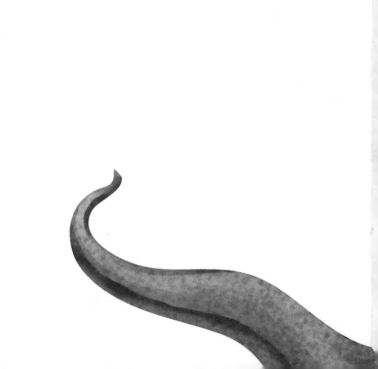